CW00521552

# A NIGHT OF ISLANDS

*Selected Poems*

PREVIOUS POETRY PUBLICATIONS BY ANGUS MARTIN

*The Larch Plantation*
*The Song of the Quern*
*Always Boats and Men* (with Mark I'Anson)


FOR PRIVATE CIRCULATION:

*The Silent Hollow*
*Rosemary Clooney Crossing the Minch*
*Laggan Days: In Memory of George Campbell Hay*
*Haunted Landscapes: Poems in Memory of Benjie*
*Paper Archipelagos*

# A Night of Islands

*Selected Poems*

ANGUS MARTIN

Edited and with a Foreword by John Killick

Poems © Angus Martin 2016

ISBN 978-1-910323-47-2

ACKNOWLEDGEMENTS

The cover illustration is based on a photograph taken at the
Galdrans, south-west Kintyre, at Summer Solstice 2011, by
James R. MacDonald, Campbeltown.

The title, *A Night of Islands*, appears in the poem 'Dancers'
and was first used by the artist Will Maclean, to whom the
poem was dedicated, in a set of ten etchings published in 1991.

Designed and typeset by Gerry Cambridge
www.gerrycambridge.com

Printed by Imprint Digital, Exeter
www.imprint.co.uk

Published by Shoestring Press
19 Devonshire Avenue, Beeston, Nottinghamshire, NG9 1BS
(0115) 925 1827
www.shoestringpress.co.uk

# Contents

III. *Ancestors & Others*

IV. *A Kintyre Nature Diary*

*Postscript*

# Foreword

It is not often that a poet of seascape and landscape has lived closer to his subjects than Angus Martin. He has worked the sea for fish and the ground for provender. He has trodden the streets and byways also to make a living. And everywhere he has gone he has been observing, annotating, comparing, especially the often impoverished present with the more plentiful past. He has done these things not primarily for poetry's sake but in response to a need to make sense of things for himself. And, astonishingly, the poems have come, all of them rich, and some of them both rich and strange.

Angus Martin is someone we believe, because when he tells us what life is like in a remote part of the Scottish mainland (Kintyre in Argyll) he knows what he is talking about. He has researched the history of the places and published prose accounts of his discoveries.

And Angus is not just a person reflecting on or recreating his experiences, he is speaking for a people, identifying with those who have suffered economic misfortune, and human persecution, in being denied their inheritance.

Make no mistake, Angus knows how to write too. The poems are vivid and memorable. They often bring us up short with a phrase or a metaphor of unusual appositeness. He evokes scenes and people with immediacy. His body of work forms an essential part of the Scottish scene, alongside that of such writers as George Campbell Hay, Iain Crichton Smith, George Bruce and George Mackay Brown. I am proud of being able to play my part in helping him to find a new audience.

JOHN KILLICK
*Editor*

# I

*Sea*

# Always Boats and Men

Always boats and men
crowding quiet vision
when I am alone
and thinking back.

Deserted harbours, ruins keeping
to themselves, the sea at evening
where fleets were crowded once,
faint chorusing of gulls.

I am seeking the one thing
to say that will say all
that is unsaid, that I may
be done with it; but there are only

images in memory
like sunlight on the sea
which is a wholeness but
broken millionfold within.

# Ten Rings in Loch Striven

Ten rings in Loch Striven
in a cold black night of teeming rain
that winter of my teens, and scarce a tail
to ease the cord of pain

that wound and tightened on my wrists
as I hung on the bar-hard back-rope,
feet to the gunnel and pitching my frame
to the boat's pitch, straining without hope.

Did I see, through tears, the summer fleets
cast off in quiet harbours and go out
to find in warm and limited darkness
the easy haul or two that brought

the needed touch? I was the boy
for romance then: it was fine to be free
on the slack of fancy's tide,
twelve years old at eight o'clock on the quay.

tail — *fish*; touch — *lucrative catch*

# Bait-gathering

That was the coldest of mornings.
My father broke ice
on the pools of the shore,
waiting for ebb.
He had gone too early,
descending the foot-sculpted stairs,
down from his attic bedroom,
bearing no light that wintry morning,
a small boy dragging a wicker creel with him.

His father stirred him,
old Duncan, squat and muscular,
smelling of tar and fish,
and for thirty years obdurate
at the helm of his own skiff,
his pride as bright to the end
as superlative yacht varnish.
His hand, as hard as barnacles,
and longer tried by common elements,
touched his son who quivered in sleep,
some innocent dream alive in him.
'It's time' was all he said.
My father woke, and time was in his mouth.
He dressed in the chill room,
and his shadow danced for him,
fantastic on a wall.

He broke ice and kicked at darkness.
His basket tipped on its side
and rocked on the bared ebb stones.
Soon he would pack it up with mussels,
with frozen hands unfastening them,
a child's tears filming his eyes,
that fisherman's son, torn from sleep,
as a living fish, in its shell of grace,
is riven from water.

# The Door

I should have saved the door.
My name was gouged in it
and 1962 the year.
My fingers could be idling at

the carvings yet, if I had kept
the surly squad in callous boots
and dust-bleached donkey-jackets
from knocking it to bits.

They drove the fish-shed down
to rubble, and all the scaly rooms
that harboured salesmen, buyers,
and stubbled loafers over drams

remarking at the dingy windows
on fishing boats that roared and swung
out of the darkness into moorings.
With reverie and scraps of song

I'd wait for the evening boats to come,
behind that door and under stairs
which might, for all I knew then,
have ended up among the stars.

# The Engineer's Kit-bag

In the canvas bag were sundry clothes,
oiled and soiled and grimed with coal-dust,
clothes asleep, bunched *heids an thraws*,
legs and arms entwined, at rest

in a throttled bag of darkness,
their bond the frame of a limited animal —
my father's frame, imprisoned on a boat,
going up and down inside compartments, his smell

and the smell of the loyal clothes
utterly the smell of compartments
in an old boat laden with coal
heading for places that made no sense

to a crouching boy with a map at his nose:
islands and sticking-out bits of the west,
the boat an invisible speck on the paper,
and his father an invisible speck on the first

speck, and the clothes on his father
invisible specks on the second speck,
and so on down to the specks
of dust and oil, of which I spoke

in the beginning, all miraculously returning,
shouldered ashore and home
by a seaman endlessly vowing
he'd quit the sea *this* time.


heids an thraws — *higgledy-piggledy*

# Air

The air is blowing round and round the world.
It must be. I've breathed this air before
and will breathe it again if I've that long
to live, and can offer

my mouth to it.
Tonight it is blowing hard;
gates and loosened bits of buildings
clatter and bang, and I've heard

enough to start me thinking
of my father's life on the sea,
and how on nights like this
I would fear for his safety,

listening in bed with a small loneliness
lying beside me, breathing as I
breathed, in perfect unison, the air
that was serenity inside, and, outside, ferocity.

# Grandfather

Grandfather's boat is out tonight.
The sea is galloping along beside her.
The sea has a simple sense of fun.
Nobody ever understood the sea.

He is an old man now, my grandfather.
Everybody thought that he was putrid.
Maybe he got restive underground.
He wanted a smoke and just got up.

The lights were strange around him,
but he sniffed the wind and came to.
He was seen determined on the trashy shore.
He was seen efficient at the fouled moorings.

The town woke up to the crack of a sail
and grandfather was steering out beyond the living,
his whiskers probing the risky dark,
antennae of an indomitable patriarch.

They are in the storm together, boat and man,
ripping water on their final voyage.
My grandfather has no mind for herrings:
he scans the smoking runs of ocean.

He forgot that he had no future.
He raised himself and shambled,
in the roaring night of a world disordered,
to the mouth of the summoning sea.

He has gone, that exceptional corpse,
at peace on an unreturning tide,
out from the land that could not hold him
and the furious howl of his grave abandoned.

# The Hird's Hoose

Yon nicht, steeved wi a sleever,
rowlin roon the Cock,
her forefut fa'in canny,
buffin seas tae smok,

A saw a licht in the Hird's Hoose
cam winkin throu the mirk
and thocht o him an his tappie doags
trachled fae thir work.

He's streetched afore a greeshach
wi the pipe sleck in his mooth,
doverin in contentment
as the gale draws tae the sooth,

but A winna hae his hirsel,
A winna tramp his hill —
gie me a lee on a boundin sea
an a toom howld tae fill.

steeved wi a sleever — *loaded with a big catch*; the Cock
(of Arran, a rock); forefut — *forefoot*; fa'in — *falling*;
buffin — *pounding*; smok — *smoke*; tappie doags — *clever dogs*;
trachled — *tired out*; greeshach — *a fire of embers*;
doverin — *drowsing*; sooth — *south*; hirsel — *flock*;
toom howld — *empty fish-hold*

# One Thousand Hooks

A trough of lines
held to his head,
not quite with the poise
of a Matabele woman;
the clop on cobbles
of his thigh-high boots
resounding in the shell
of a frosted morning.

His wife, at the click
of the door's closing,
woke, and her vision filled
with a glistening blue torment of mussels,
each with a hissing mouth
that wanted opened;
and her hands wore rags again,
swathing only cold and pain.

One thousand baited hooks
and a bounding sea to try them in —
O, come to our hidden steel
you mouths that are invisible
when Sanda's open on the Ru'
and dawn with its fraying strings of fire
plays on the sleeping hills of Ayrshire.

# Out with the Coastguard 1

*On the recovery of a body at Tangytavil shore, Kintyre,*
*23 October 1986*

As we turned the drowned Irishman
into the disinfected
body-bag at six-thirty this evening, the light was going.

The third of four lost men,
he was long in the body,
his hair red, and a ring
on a finger with a costly stone
set within it, lustreless.

Mostly I remember the huge sky,
sweeping night with it,
and the stridence of the cold sea.

# Who Among Common Men
## of their Time?

Who among common men of their time
could claim such freedom? They had their boats
and could catch a wind to hell and back
and spit in the storm's black eye
from a lee of their ancestry.

And money? They had it or hadn't.
The pleuter of herring or stroke of a wandering solan
in some still bight with dusk on the water
and *there* was the flurry of notes
equal in every man's hand
and a stroke of ink through every debt-line.

You could ask them the name of a rock,
the shape of the ground
five fathoms under the keel,
the meaning of this or that in nature's order,
and you'd have your answer, aye,
more than you'd asked for.

pleuter — *splash*; stroke — *plummet*; solan — *gannet*

# Herring Scales

When there was a fishing worth
mentioning on this coast,
when nobody noticed it was there
because it had been there
since the big-fisted ancestors
fumbled English,
herring scales were the real coinage.

They stuck to everything:
door-knobs, seaboots, oilskins,
plates and mugs, wood-handled knives
and sometimes when I open an old book
that lived its useful days at sea
I find again their tarnished silver,
the tokens of lost times.

# The Banks o Ballantrae

We slew a michty nation on the Banks o Ballantrae,
McCrindle an McCreath an Sloan wir there.
We got nae sleep for near three week
wi landin spannie herrin intae Ayr.

The winter fishin maks ye gled o herbours,
but only if there's time tae hae a doss.
When ye're aff yer feet, it's time tae eat
and if yer heid gaes doon the grub's yer only loss.

For mony a wan haes slep' face tae the table,
hale crews in scaly boots an skins awa
intae that blissful warld where there's nae herrin,
nae boats, nae buyers, naethin real at a.

An if ye haena got a shot tae haud ye at the quay
fillin endless baskets fae the howld,
as sure as Hell ye'll hae a spell
o mendin nets oot in the freezin cowld.

For the Banks is where the damage is —
the grun's gey sair on gear —
an ye'll hae tae stan wi needle in han
an steek up ilka teir.

But, och, we'll thole it a, boys, an scowrie weather tae,
for we ken that Setterday's aye drawin near.
Wi a dirty sheaf o nots in yer nefe
ye'll droon the Banks o Ballantrae in beer.


*for Bob Smith*


michty — *mighty*; spannie — *spawning*; gled — *glad*; haud — *hold*;
howld — *(fish-)hold*; grun — *ground*; sair — *sore*;
steek up ilka teir — *stitch up every tear*; scowrie — *rough*; nefe — *fist*

# The Captains

1

What is it out there that could
freeze you now, draw a sweaty film
on your palms and bug your eyes?
Only the living, by God, the living,
unmet, unfathomed to a man
where the inky hills are in their
old proportions and hissing ridges
of the water loom between the shores.
Who is out there? No one that you know,
captains, so cry in the night:
'What ship, and where bound?'
All bound where you are come from.


2

Loitering, aimless, at the Weigh-house,
a storm on the roof of the
bulking Christian Institute
beyond MacEachern's memorial cross,
a mediaeval intricacy of stone,
heavenward mystery uncommented on
over the clash of rigging and the lash
of harboured waves. The captains
pace in blue among the casual
knots of crew, pausing to train an eye
on the black well of the weather,
and almost — almost — saying: 'We'll go home.'

3

Receiving the captains into my home
required no preparation; they came
with the gait of men accustomed
to straddling water on the thin
comfort of drunken planking,
and rolled themselves politely through the door.
There was whisky for one hand and cake
for the other, and a window beyond
the clock face and the hanging light,
and they gathered there before the glass
seeing themselves reflected, and remembering
the outer space of wind and sea.


4

Let me shake your hands. Goodbye, captains.
Be careful out there, where you are bound.
Perhaps you have forgotten certain dangers —
fingers of gloomy shore and the sunken teeth of reefs —
and remember there are new lights everywhere.
You'll manage, I dare say, but do not tell me where
you're going, or I may wish to go with you,
a passenger just — no skills to serve you with —
sitting below, hearing the tongues of the sea
and the creaking of the skiff's old bones,
a boy in the bilgy dark, hunched at a mug of tea,
far from home, my captains, very far from home.


*for Tomas Tranströmer*

# The Ship

## 1

The ship has come back to the forest
the ship that is curious about ancestry
has sailed by the harbours that clasped her in storm
the yard where she rose from the spine of a keel
the sawmill that sundered the corpses of giants;
the ship has returned to the forest
sure on the course of the one true death
and see how she glides on an ocean of leaves
over the depths of unfelled destinies.


## 2

The ship has come back to the forest
seeking a grave for herself
where sunlight is dry and land is more
than a glimpse through mist and rain
or a memory pitched on an ocean of voyaging;
and here in the forest a native peace
has soothed her chafed and weary strakes;
her sails slip down, a last undressing;
shrouds and stays, as their tension goes,
sag, and she is ready at last to lie over —
deep in the sunless forest of kin —
to an end without salt or fire.

# The Tiller

I am dark and smooth, polished by many hands,
but the one hand that I loved has gone,
so let me swing to the rudder's motion,
moored in the lee, alone.

I knew the change of weather by his grip
and felt his hunter's passion like a tide,
and the herring scales he rubbed on me
were jewels that I wore with pride.

I pitied him when wind and rain
pressed him, huddling to steer,
up against my nakedness,
the only language we could share.

There's not a man in all Kintyre
will point me to the open sea;
I'll bear no other master's hand,
but burn instead — unship me.

# The Mast

The horizontal — death to you.
When I saw you laid
in the muck and clutter of the quay
I knew that you were dead.

Not broken, split or flawed
that I could see, but unstepped
from mother deck and slung ashore
ungainly on a hook, you who leapt

at stars and rocked your head
over the surge of running seas,
or gentle on smooth sunlit waters
quietly nodded, upright and at ease.

Your grave is by the fish-shed,
under the lost, unmourning sky,
and only perching gulls will mind
your sea-years gone by.

# Tonight the Fleets

Tonight the fleets are on the water.
Every boat that ever sailed
out to the fields of herring
cuts a burning furrow
in the living phosphorescence
of the powering ridges.
The fields are greeny water;
their crops are keen and glancing.

What are those voices
that thread the darkness?
The seabirds snap them
in the air, like thin wires
taut across the centuries:
the Gaelic of the buried men
of Minard, Tarbert, Carradale,
and the guttural Scots of Campbeltown.

Their graves are opened up this night,
the rough-walled yards disgraced
by upheaved earth, and headstones
overthrown and shattered,
their lists of dead obliterated.
But no one saw the steady march
of cheerful bands to the old harbours
crammed by craft that had gone for kindling.

No one saw — no one remained
to see, and every light was out.
There was an end of culture, history,
and an end to the burial of dead.
How could those good men sleep on such a night?
Perhaps there will be herring caught again,
and nets hung up to dry, and weather watched...
but tonight they merely try their hands.

# Dancers

I am the boy who grew
like a limpet stuck to the quay.
I saw boats and fishermen
dancing on the sea.

And I wished that I could dance
in a yellow oilskin suit,
dance on the dancing water
to the slap of an old thigh-boot.

They were champions of some greater dance
performed in a night of islands;
O, show me your faces like grimy charts
and lay on my head your barnacled hands,

for I fear you have danced your passage
into the ports of the ground.
But I watch for your gull-haloed coming —
the limpet sticks around.


*for Will Maclean*

# Sea Stories

I sang in a pub last night.
I sang for the man I am,
the place that I was born
and the people I was raised among.

I had forgotten that I still
belong where tales go round
the whisky-gilded table
and silences offend.

The company was fishermen,
fashioned to the sea;
I moved their masks aside
and saw that they were really

far from land and searching
the lost years of the tales,
old men on the shifting edge
of dangerous essentials.

# II

## *Land*

# This Land of Mine

This land of mine voided its children
and cast a language
on to foul middens
at the ends of roofless houses
on cold coasts and windy hills.

Remote, this inheritance of stone.
Like endless threads
in an aerial
tapestry
the white fanning tracks
of the transatlantic jets
are strung above it.

At twenty thousand feet a human hand
could obliterate all this.
Through the bottom
of a whisky glass
held to a fuddled eye
this would be nothing.

That old man may be a ghost
if there are ghosts to be found
here or elsewhere.
He is walking to a distant
geometrical puzzle of earth,
a stamp of green
on an envelope of twisted heath.
His father sent messages to some god
that nobody any longer cares to remember:
'Give us corn and potatoes plentifully
this year — amen.'

Rain permeated the ethnic roof cover,
dripping on cattle and people

without discrimination,
a Japanese torture perfected
in a Gaelic labour-camp.
And when the storm rushed down the roof-hole,
a sooty demon,
they laughed among themselves, debating
the lexical variations
of *tuberculosis* in Gaelic.
Their stories took so long in telling
around peat-fires that were invented
to lend adornment to history,
that nobody could think of leaving.
They were detained by the richness of a culture.

# Field History

And people lived here, humans
I tell you; children were born
and children died in this wet
hole in the rock; but a fire would burn

night and day, I suppose,
of wood thrown at their feet
by these same waves you see out there...
or ancestors of theirs, at any rate.

They ate from the sea, too —
imagine the ocean as a great plate
feeding those prowling destitutes,
only it didn't put much fat

on them. A diet of *wilks*
and *gleshans* was hardly the ultimate
in rich living. Still, of those
that survived you couldn't have met

a hardier lot, I was assured
by old Bob Wylie who set creels
for crab and lobster
long ago down this shore. He calls

this place the Wee Man's Cove.
Notice the drystone wall
for breaking wind and rain
at the cave mouth, and sadly that's all

that remains of them, boys and girls,
unless we consider the hidden
end of all things material,
and that's it over there — the midden.

wilks — *winkles*;  gleshans — *small saithe*

# Places

## 1. *Place-names*

I am the sole heir to maybe
a hundred place-names snatched
from the cooling brains of farmers
and fishermen who have since fitted
neatly into holes dug for them
in a few places beginning with *Cill.*

To have moved among multitudes
of names, strewing hill and shore —
the bones of a great language
that perished in remoteness —
and to lie in death with a solitary name
tagged on the final place of all:

such is the narrowing of choice.

## 2. *Places*

I get friendly towards places
that are kind to me — liberal
with sunlight, intolerant
of winds — and there is an inescapable

satisfaction in knowing
that the dead of my family
were also on good terms
with these enduring places, whose duty

appears to be the reception
of us brains-on-forks:
tramping about, excreting,
littering, and constantly releasing facts

and opinions that go up into the air
or maybe travel over the sea
like a host of winged insects
intense in their day.


## 3. *Empty Places*

Why do empty places trouble us?
Is it that the small
persistent intimations of mortality
wait out there to draw us?
A burnished fox that points its brush at nothing;
a wailing buzzard rounding on the wind;
a raven blackening a crag with waiting.

Is it that the people vanished?
Camp out there alone for days
attuned to wind and water only,
those tireless forces that attend
the greater motion of what men
still hesitate and call 'eternity',
and you will hear the unexpected:
people's voices, tugged and torn
to scattered syllables, drifting on
beyond you in the bearing wind.

But are they 'real'?
I tell you, everything is real
out there, when you are stopped alone
on a broken ridge of jumbled stone
and the sky is the only traveller.

# Grass

That stalk of brittle mountain grass —
paled by the chilly suck of winter —
is caught in the carpet fibres yet.
If it had brains it wouldn't know
what to do with them.
Anyway, its root is stuck elsewhere
in a hard place for grass and all.
That stalk got here in someone's boot.
Grass seldom travels far except in the guts of animals.
Nobody seems to want to be kind to grass.

Last night, I swear, I heard the song of grass
here in this room, a song I'd heard before
one evening I was walking
with stones and sand in my pockets
and the cold stare of the moon
imperious over my left shoulder.

By the strayed effulgence of a dream
I looked about, and suddenly
I was walking far at sea
through roving meadows of the sunlight
shaking and hissing all the way to Antrim.

# Wood

Concerning the history of wood,
the sea has much to say
in its many vying voices.
But the sea is no judge of wood,
knowing only the broken ends of trees,
and trees have no notion of the sea —
their birth is small in earth;
their faith goes straight to the sun.

Wood may journey in its death only,
blind on the back of the ocean,
night and day through a hell of water.
Trees are noble, lonely things
that passion cannot touch.
Songbirds visit them with passion,
but the ocean birds look down on trees,
pitching far at sea, and pass.

All wood returns to land,
to rot in graves of sand or gravel
or stand grotesque in a waste of rocks,
lodged for the wind to warp and powder,
in death still monumentally
trees, but bare and birdless.
Hear out the history of sundered wood,
told in the mouth of the rootless sea.

# Forest

Since I lately came to live
in an old house with a fire in it,
wood has got into my vision.

I put my saw to wood
and glance a nick, and then I cut
wood into bits that please me.

Weight and form may please me,
and I am pleased to own
what at last I have to burn.

I am a Scottish wood-collector;
I belong to a great tradition
of bleeding hands and thick coats.

Wood accumulates about me;
I build it into piles,
I bag it and I lug it.

I love the look of wood:
its surfaces are maps and pictures
and staring eyes and voiceless mouths.

Wood to the end is unresisting:
it lets me lift and drag it
far from the place that it lay down.

Wood will never fight
the blade's truncating stroke
or scream when fire consumes it.

But I had dreams of wood.
I was alone in a high forest,
sun and seasons banished.

The trees bent down their silent heads
and closed their branches round about
and I was gathered into air.

I burn in my dreams of wood,
a melting torch suspended
in the dark heart of a silent forest.

*for Sid Gallagher*

# Malcolm MacKerral

MacKerral, that was one hard winter.
Your father died on the moor road,
his bag of meal buried under snows.
Death relieved him of his load.

Raking wilks with freezing fingers,
your little sisters crawled the shore,
scourged by gusting showers
until their knees were raw and sore.

Your few black cattle, thin and famished,
lay and died at the far end
of the draughty common dwelling.
There was little else you owned.

In the factor's oaken-panelled room
that the shafting sunlight glossed
you looked for your reflection:
you had become a ghost.

That month a stranger entered
the green cleft of the glen.
You watched him coming, from a hill,
and stabbed the earth again.

When he returned he brought the sheep.
At the house where you were born
you closed a door behind you.
Two hundred years had gone.

There was no end to the known land.
You looked, and there were names
on every shape around you.
The language had its homes.

Words had their lives in rivers;
they coursed them to the sea.
Words were great birds on mountains,
crying down on history.

Words were stones that waited
in the silence of the fields
for the voices of the people
whose tenures there had failed.

You knew those names, MacKerral;
your father placed them in your mouth
when language had no tragic power
and you ran in your youth.

You ran in the house of the word
and pressed your face upon the glass
and watched the mute processions
of your grave ancestors pass.

Look back on what you cannot alter.
Not a stone of it is yours to turn.
All that you leave with now:
lost words for the unborn.

# In Memory of Robert McInnes, Died 3 July, 1987

## 2. *At the Peat Bank*

The time of cutting came and went — you were not there;
the time of 'changing' came and went — you were not there;
the time of gathering came and went — you were not there.

Where shall I find you now,
in the forests of the lost sheep-hills?

In the hollow where we'd sit,
year after year, facing the one way,
to eat and sup at tea, and slice obligatory plug,
as black and oily as the third peat down,
I looked for you, but there was no impression
to mark the patience of your weight.

Flies buzzed; the skylarks twittered on the thin
wires of their communications with infinity,
and that's it: you're somewhere out there,
rolling up your sleeves, spitting on your hands,
and smiling — your face the face of a boy to the end —
under the glare of an endless noon
on the moors that will never let you go home.

# In Memory of John Campbell, Died 17 July 1987

We've seen the last of the 'Snake Man'.
Hills and roads that knew his tread, mourn
for John MacFadyen Campbell
whose stomach filled with blood and bile.

I have it from a serpent's mouth
that John is happy in the earth;
his coffin is a little hole
that looks on neither heaven nor hell.

He frequented the snaky places —
rocks and dykes — and fixed his prizes
sure to the ground on a stick's
forked end, always able for their antics.

Vain prisoners, they would never eat
in the house of man, and he would let
them go when he was satisfied
with watching them. No serpent died

in Campbell's keeping, and when he was too old
to reach their haunts, he held
converse with the woodlice in his walls
and fed the birds and lifted snails

out of the path of heedless feet.
Now he has got the weight
of destiny upon him, that no one
may rise from under, and the known

sum of all his life is just
a sudden rumouring in trees, a lost
movement in the corner of an eye;
and he is quartered where the serpents lie.

# Mountain Roads

There are roads that no one travels
out on the spurned mountains.
The mountains are hard to the heart;
their memories are shed in streams
and are the food of dark-coloured fish,
stunted but proud
in the shade of leaning banks.
The eyes of the fish see a world
small and familiar to the last stone.

The mountains see nothing
and cannot celebrate their greatness.
Men marked the mountains:
ditched and drained and walled them,
dug the black and secret peat,
and bared their tracks.
Nobody went to the rock.
They stopped before the rock:
who would make a labour
hewing mountain
when all its broken
open faces lumped the fields,
a curse on tillage?

The roads are hiding now,
but under grass and bracken
the roads go wandering
lured by a moon that no one sees
rising big and calm
over the blue and silent
rise of mountains.
The moon makes its song
of stone to the stone
of the rooted mountains,
but the men are dead

who swung in the tide
of the evening's muted air
and through the waves of silence
heard the moon's
solemn song to sibling stone.

Yes, the roads go wandering,
rippling air.
Where do they go?
They go where they have always gone,
to the places people laid
their mortal shadows on.
But the roads are lonely everywhere.
They pass the scattered stones
that stood for houses;
the fields that rocked with corn,
sunk in greedy rushes now;
the peat-banks that lay bare for yield,
mere pits of shadow now.

The roads are lonely in their journeys.
There was an end to voices
some time that is far
back in the time of roads,
and an end to feet
treading them, defining them.
A road without travellers
is a sad road,
but the roads have pride.
They wander by themselves
and meet where they have always met,
when the moon is a distant face
lighting up the empty lands.

*for Bob Smith*

# Peat

The mountains wear a dark flesh:
cold and damp and dead,
deep to the gravel lining bedrock,
and the great sculpted bone
of the mountain's being,
the essential mountain itself,
bulking rock rooted down
in the drifting rock of the world.

People toiled out there
on the sunny mountain flank.
They cut the flesh of the mountain
and fed it to their fires.
Their voices keep in brittle kernels
sunk in the silent peat pack,
like the barren nuts of hazel
that fell in an age of forests
and lay to the dour advance
of chill entombing bog.

Crack the shells and you will hear
a careless note of laughter
or a word or two from a wasted tongue
or the broken end of an old song
drifting from you.

# III

*Ancestors & Others*

# Ancestors

All these people at my back,
watching me — out there —
people clothed in animal skins
and others only in body hair,

half animals themselves, poking me with sticks
in the soft parts of my unconscious,
startling me with sudden mad cries
and eliciting responses

that escape my knowledge
let alone my understanding.
I have been waking lately
in the middle of dreams, demanding

explanation, but they are secretive
and sly, and slide their sticks
under my bed and slink
along the walls, their shadowy backs

eluding me. But sometimes I will
lie awake and catch them unawares,
crouched in the middle of my room,
shielding small fires.

# Antrim

Today snow came from Antrim
in an odd light: beams of filmy orange,
confused and shifting imperceptibly,
fingered out from a cloud chase.

On clearer days, from hills south,
I have seen fields and houses
defined on a swell of land
miles across pitching water.

And a man who died when I
was a mere unheeding boy
saw from the height of Knock Moy
in the eye of a pocket telescope

season upon season a white
and solitary horse in a certain field
of Antrim draw a plough
until a time came round

when horse and ploughman
broke no earth, and then he knew
that nothing moves unchanging
on the land that is eternal.

Today I looked on Antrim
and history was in my eyes;
I saw the horse and the horseman
appear on a screen of snow

that came from the west and Ireland
as my people came in another time,
like that driven snow landfalling
on destiny and dissolution.

# Aunt

We quarrelled years ago about
inscriptions on a stone above a grave
that you no longer may attend
with flowers and a lugubrious hat;
but when I saw you lately
I could have cried with shame
that my wilful pride and pettiness
had kept me from your home.

You are a woman done,
and the world will soon be done of you:
white hair unwashed and stiffening
about a grey collapsing face,
and your body frail as an old stuffed heron
crumbling in the glass of a grim museum
that nobody cares to visit any more.

You cannot leave your bed now
and your smell has made the room
undoubtedly your very own.
I thought that I smelt death there,
but it may have been that guilt of mine
oozing from every pore of me
because I was remembering,
as I turned my back on you
and stood at a quiet familiar window,
that you were my father's sister.

You'll have a stone yourself soon,
above your quiet head,
and there will be no disputation:
who quarrels with the dead?

# Uncle

You dropped into the water
and held yourself erect
all the way down to the point
at which death met you.

The note you left in the
lodging-house was for
your mother only,
and whatever cry she found
pressed between its folds
she took into herself
and locked it there, an echo
in an Irish strong-box.

So what unmoored you,
what storm of introspection
drove you out from harbour
and into the pull of some
unseen magnetic darkness?
Lean fishings, and no hope of coin
on the last-chance Greenock gravel boats;
the wrong love of a Stranraer shop-girl?

We all have a photograph of you,
handsome and dressed to shame a gentleman,
your subtle mouth, in reproductions,
endlessly inviting water.

# Encampment at the Inans

Sentiment — a grease on the mind.
I break the film and find your face beneath it.
Sun-flashings on the slack skin of the Atlantic;
moonlight filling a small tent —
you woke to it, but I slept on.

Between the stations of sun and moon
we walked together on the string of a bay,
the sea playing it, an old song.
We were in the two lights,
but which of us could make the choice:
sun or moon? Another light leapt on the shore,
a fire of driftwood gathered from
the legacy of winter's tides.

We sat on the blackest rock and watched
a light coming and a light going,
and the lesser light that would remain
for as long as we could give it force.

We left in the heat of the day after,
the sun a raging tyrant — inescapable —
and the moon as faded as an old dead moth
cold in the ash of a done fire.


*for Judy*

# Four for Sarah

1

Why do you drop stones in the water?
You are my daughter and I have to know,
seeing I aid you in the matter.
Where do you think they go?

They go to the bottom of your mind,
I think, and stir some ancient sediment
of peaceful things that graced the sand
once, and that's why you're content

to drop stones in the water
day after day, somebody's daughter
a thousand years ago or more,
stooped and silent on the same shore.

2

You notice the smallest things in the world
that human eyes can see,
because you are very small yourself
and pay no mind to me.

I was intent on the big things
until you made me see
a bubble at risk on the ocean,
a leaf hanging on to a tree.

3

From whom did you learn to laugh so?
Not from me, I'm sure,
unless you caught some echo
of the child I am no more.

Your laughter lifts me like a cloud
gathering for rain;
I float in its pure suspension,
then fall to earth again.


4 *(for her asleep)*

I have brought you blaeberries
from a mountain far away
that you may taste the sweetness
gathered from this day.

Each berry holds a moment
your little mouth will break;
the blueness of the mountain
shall mark you when you wake.

# Dalintober

There are evenings when I feel like walking round Dalintober,
usually when the light is gentle and patient,
encouraging the character of things to emerge.

The place is friendly to me,
like an old dog curled on the hearth of the loch,
but its tail never wags.
Its tail is the old stone quay,
and there is no life to move it
since the fishermen became extinct.

I used to meet the fishermen there
when I was drunk and rambling
in the dark after closing-time.
I wanted to meet them
and I suppose that's why
they dutifully appeared,
their intricately woven jerseys —
wrought on four needles, seamless —
so deep a blue that night
absorbed them. But I saw the faces
shining like new bone
or ivory, every feature hewn
out of the whiteness of the moon.

I recognised a few of them
from tired pictures. Some,
my ancestors, were kind to me,
spitting discreetly and opening
each his battered *spleuchan*,
an offer I was always able to refuse.
They never spoke to me,
but stood apart,
their faces white and rapt
in helpless scrutiny.

I imagine now they puzzled
why I had brought them back.
Always they gazed around them
stiffly like statues waking
baffled on anchoring plinths.
They looked beyond the quay and saw
no skiffs at moorings, darkly
nodding their wearied prows,
hard wenches in a dream
of slain herrings.
They looked to the land and saw
impossible architecture
bulk where their homes had been.

They'd shuffle and turn their eyes from me,
uneasy with ancient debts
to times vacated,
and I would leave them then
to wander back alone
glimpsing heredity, small
in the eye of ruin:
sea-walls with mooring rings intact;
the stumps of net-poles
rotting in the ebb;
boot-sculpted slabs descending into water;
street corners where they'd gather
in the lee of weather,
notching out an edge of stone
honing knives.


*for my daughter Sarah Campbell, b. 22.8.1987*


spleuchan – *tobacco-pouch*

# My Pet Flint-knapper

My pet flint-knapper is becoming
vicious. He doesn't like houses
and he doesn't like me.
He's trying to tell me
but I cannot understand his words,
though I understand the white-knuckled
nodule that he brandishes
excitedly when I approach too near.

I found him under a bare hill
on a windless day last week,
lonely beside the blackened hearth
of a dead fire, his flints in a grubby leather bag:
all that he had in the world.

He ran away at once when I appeared
but he'd left his bag in haste
and soon returned. I gestured 'food'
and he followed me suspiciously
grunting and girning in that way of his.

The invitation didn't work.
I should have known that he was too
much a stranger to be happy here.
He stinks in his skins, throws down uneaten food
on the floor and will only shit
in the garden with the stray dogs
I detest and drive away.

I believe he finds them more companionable —
his words with them are gentle and his hands
exhibit tenderness. I'm half-hoping now
that he'll go off with them before
the anthropologists arrive.

# MacMillan's Dog

MacMillan was dead when his boat
spun slowly on her keel at the rock,
lay to the surge of the breakers,
then tilted. He didn't come out,
but a half-starved dog came out,
limping and whimpering
and clattering its chain on the gravel.
It dragged itself into a wood,
with many backward glances to the sea.

Here's to MacMillan who was a steady fisherman
and a whisky-smuggler of some distinction
intimate with every bight between
Port a' Chruidh and Bagh mu Dheas,
and here's to the dog, his faithful servant,
that was never right in the head again,
and dragged its chain through the woods of Lagan
barking at owls.


*for Imala Kullos*

# Passchendaele

Hae ye cam here fae Passchendaele?
Close-mooth tae stair-heid's a trail o glar.
Ye look lik a man's been deid owerlang,
still rug in a kilt for the war.

Forgie me — A'll no invite ye in.
It's no that A'm prood o the hoose
or asham't o ma granfaither, no:
it's the state o yer claes, an yer boose.

Ye'd frichten the weans if they saw ye,
an A'm tellin ye truthfully noo —
A'm jeest a bit feart o yer look, masel,
an the guff o ye gies me the grue.

Ah weel, ye willna speak, or canna.
That A'll dae, an mair, masel.
Here's ma han — Hoo ir ye, man,
an hoo ir things in Hell?

There is nae Hell? — Ye're talkin noo!
Hell's where ye went tae dee,
blawn tae smoorach bi a shill
in the blinkin o an ee.

But ye've got yer body back thegither —
it's taen ye mair as seeventy year —
an ye're lookin for yer faimily
an tryin tae gaither up yer gear.

But we divna want tae think on war;
we haena got wan on ee noo.
We're leevin weel an sweir tae feel
aucht o the blast that ruint you.

There's aye a wheen o wars gan on
aroon the warld, an aye will be;
it's jeest yer luck if ye get struck
an sunnert fae yer faimily.

There's no a wan that minds o' ye
an no a wan that cares,
sae bide a ghaist an lee us be:
A'll see ye doon the stairs.

*In memory of John Mackenzie, 1888–1917*

glar — *mud*; owerlang — *overlong*; boose — *scowl*;
guff — *stink*; hoo — *how*; smoorach — *fragments*;
ee noo — at present; sweir — *reluctant*; aucht — *anything*;
wheen — *number*; gan — *going*; sunnert — *sundered*;
ghaist — *ghost*; lee — *leave*

# Shores

A sadness drifts on the shores,
a mist, this evening, and it is alive
with phantoms, and whether I have put them there
or not will make no difference.

Bereavement glooms the shores:
herrings, gannets, whales and men
have lost their seasons,
and nature's broken wheel
lies toppled, each slow turn
wearing down the axis.

Lodan, Machrie, Catacol,
Airde Bhaine and Grianan,
Sgolaig, Lagan, Cour...

Yes, you have your names;
you lived in tradition's living mouth,
as real in the moment of the naming
as wives and children gathered to recall
when pipes were filled in the timber-creaking
dens of the herring-hunting skiffs,
plunging at anchor far from home,
a wind of North shrill in the rigging.

They spoke of you, I think, as loved ones,
belonging in the calm light of their youth —
the summer fishings of the shore,
tents and fires in every bight,
and boats at ease on sagging cables,
night horses tethered in the sun.

Who knows you now and who remembers?
Who touches on your slender bodies
and promises to touch again? I swear,
all who were your lovers in the herring years

are dead and gone, and you are only names,
as dead as they, for what it matters,
when evenings cruel with evocation
bring a stillness to the hills
and nothing moves upon the waters.


*for Neil Short*

# Below Zero

When Campbell was going home
by the moor way to his shepherd's hut,
swaggering and drunk from the fair,
and haranguing a deaf audience
of frost-glittering stars,
his fuddled senses failed him.

He did not know that Death
was on his trail, and caught him
on the mountainside, saying:
'Here — you're mine now:
let me dust this white stuff
over you while you sleep.'

# The Buried

I wonder how many people
are buried in Kintyre without
a memorial of any kind
over them, and if the lack
would matter to some of them
were they able to take a step
out of time and look at the ground
containing their dust but no
label of contents.

I know this: there are more people
unmarked than marked through millennia
of inhumations, but where exactly are they all
and what do they look like now?
Mostly they look like the earth itself,
and perhaps the potatoes and carrots
you ate today contained
infinitesimally the physical residue
of a flintknapper
or a Pict who was cut down
under a still and blood-red sky
when the thousand-miles-travelled rollers
beat the drum of their own extinction
on the bay of Machrihanish
and sent a tribute of salt
into the swamplands of Laggan.

But don't stop eating potatoes and carrots —
there may be brains inside roots and tubers,
and perhaps a grain of another style
of experience will enter your chemistry
and on a screen in the dream-
laboratory you will watch
a flint nodule in the slowed-down

process of disintegration,
and, immediately after,
a sword will chop 'you' into bits
and you won't ever know which
were the flakes of the nodule
and which were the flakes of you.

# Erradil

### 1

There is snow with the last of the sunlight
coming down through the neck of the glen,
and my pockets are heavy with shards
of china, each glaze-veined
with the dark earth's ageing.

Amelia, Amelia, Amelia MacKay –
I return your name to the stone mounds
and the greening fields as smooth as plates,
feeding only sheep now.

I came here to speak your name,
you who broke through to the world
here, and grew to be a woman,
strong-limbed, industrious, beautiful;
and from the broken earth about the walls
I gathered these mementoes,
the spillage of ancestral middens.

Here is a curved, blue-patterned
rim fragment of a drinking bowl;
perhaps your young girl's lips were on that bowl
when someone called you from the fire
and startled you,
'Amelia! Amelia!'

### 2

I crave an intimacy with my great-great-great grandmother.
It is a perverse desire and will quickly pass.
I shouldn't be confessing any of this,
but today I sat by the shell of her birthplace,

a hill farm nobody speaks of any more;
night was closing in, and minimal snow salted the cold land.
I saw the houses rebuild themselves
and the roofs draw thatch from the rush thickets;
fires within sent plumes to their cloud-gods;
cattle lowed, and children bickered in shrill voices.

A woman came out and saw me sitting quietly.
She was lovely in her surprise and asked my name.
Her name, she said, was Amelia MacKay.
When I told her I came of her blood
and was folded in a dream out of my time,
she smiled and led me to a bed of straw.

3.

Today I returned to Erradil,
drawn by a distant cloud of sails —
a ghost ship cresting hills, with its compass needle
tense and trembling on west.

It is the ship of the dead, and swings to an anchor now
on the smooth grazings where barley once
stirred in golden waves to the wind:
'The heaviest barley ever known to go into Campbeltown.'

The dead are wading through the green water—
laughing, glad, and all as one again—
to the rubble island that was home,
and a guiding light on the land swells.

Now I shall go, and leave them to their time,
fearing that I too shall become a ghost,
thinned to a spirit with my own kin,
but adrift still, beyond their recognition.

*for my daughter, Amelia Agnes, b. 11.8.1989*

# Ghosts

I have developed a strong attachment to the ghosts.
I love them, and let them come to my fire
and sit out their evenings, smoking and spitting,
waiting for night, that they may resume
the business of being dead.

They have not taken death
lying down — that much I understand
from ghosts. They crave activity,
and while we sleep are busy
visiting the emotional power-points

of their former lives on earth.
They plug in and are young again —
such visions that flock to them!
Be careful in your lives and do not
alter or destroy the power of ghosts,

which is stored mainly in buildings, but can also be
found in shady hollows of the hills,
in trees festooned with the invisible
streamers of children's laughter,
or on the bright shores of vanished summers.

Most of my ghosts were fishermen.
Their names are known to me, and one was in love
with a sister of my great-great grandfather.
They haunt the sea, in preference to land,
which renders them harmless in conventional

superstition, unless you happen to be in a boat
when night falls on a stream of power out there.
But they are powerless themselves, content to drift
over the shores that once rang with their cries,
as nets came in, seething with silver of herring.

They see distant lights, and the dim shape of sail and hull
passing, hear the whale blow and smell her stink
on the wind, and gaze below to the phosphorescent screen
of the water, that flickers messages no longer clear
to them, for they are circling aloft, great silent birds.

# IV

*From a Kintyre*
*Nature Diary*

# Three Hundred Geese

Three hundred geese got up
and shot their practised arrows
over the foraged fields
of Laggan late this evening.

This will be goodbye to geese,
goodbye.

They beat away on a wind of spring
and will forget that they were ever here,
that gaggling host

loud from the bow of instinct.

*

# Toad

The fawn-backed inch-long toad
leapt from the threat of my tread
and clung on a clump of blueberry
watching with one impassive eye
for what the never before encountered
thing would do next.

I the thing did nothing but
imitate his watchfulness
then tiring of the game
before he did
left him lordly on his bush
to cleanse my useless image from his brain.

# The Larch Plantation

When the north wind forays
among the larches —
greener than all the greens assembled here —
I hear the sound of water boiling,
but really it's only the wind
stirring surfaces as the sun travels north.

*

# Islands

Islands are bits of the land
that prefer their own company,
recluses that sea and wind
address in peculiar accents.

*

# The Dyke-builders

Do not, in death, desert your monuments —
I'll place a rock in the gap
of an ageing dyke beyond
the kiln of Lossit, and trust you

to foregather and repair the rest
one morning when you'll startle
sheep along the sun-pierced wall,
gazing from one world through to another

# Crossbill

Where you came to be killed
was far enough from a pine forest:
a window-pane that stopped you
in your flight — a thud, and then
the after-motion of some
downy feathers floating.

There was no dying for you —
a broken neck extinguished life
at once. I took you home and laid you
in a volume opened at the photograph
of *Crossbill, 15 cm., p.698*: that's you.

The girls came home and charily
stroked your breast; a lad who studies birds
later arrived and looked you over.

Now you and I are quite alone.
This is a house and you're not seeing it.
That's a clock and you're not hearing it.

Rather you here than I in a forest
tonight with the snow falling noiselessly
into the trees that will never miss you.

\*

# Swans

Over the black harbour waters
dazzling swans glide
each a hissing serpent lodged
in the trousseau of a bride.

## The Lone Rowan

The lone rowan with head bowed east
cannot see the alien spruce
congregated at her back,
heads erect and scanning for
the lost sun of Japan.

*

## The Wind

The wind cannot find me
here in this pine-girt hollow;
he tries low-prowling
but the tallest grasses and rushes
quake to his touch and I see him.
I see him too above me
circling in the highest trees
a blind beast
strong with emptiness.

*

## Permanent Animal

Bright days are full of hill and shore.
The true purpose of being out there:
to halt frequently and breathe
like a permanent animal,
and to look with the eyes
of a permanent animal
into the moment
that has halted too.

# Scart, Kilchousland

Black scart on a black rock
perched in pelting rain,
for fifteen minutes only
I should like to have your brain
installed within a part of mine
to analyse your every thought
or maybe there would only be
one image — of a fish you'd caught;
and you could have this brain of mine
one minute only of its strife
lest in that tide of dark confusion
you lost the compass of your life.

*

# Grianan

It was just the particular position
I'd stopped in afforded a novel view
of the little hill's familiar crown
gleaming green from earlier rain
and crowded with slender dappled cattle
I'd say had gathered there to wear
the final hours of sunlight on their skin.

*

# These Fine Memories

These fine memories are as ferns
of pale-green fragility growing
at the back of the darkness
in dank and dripping shore-caves
persistent in minimal light.

# Lamb

Back today at the Inans —
a kind of pilgrimage
to a loved and distant bay —
I walked straight into horror:
a plump lamb with the eyes
half-stabbed from his head.
Out, I thought at first,
seeing the arc of blood
he'd smeared around him on the grass,
casting his head from side to side.

I tried to raise him on his legs,
but he couldn't stand, and flopped again,
mutely writhing, bewildered and afraid.
I had intruded on
the manner of his dying,
but I couldn't let him be.
I held his head and looked:
the sockets were not robbed,
or not entirely, but blood congealing
masked the wounds.
I fetched him water in a dish
out of the gully of Allt Dubh —
pure water from the mountain —
but he refused to drink.

And the sudden forms of hoodie
and black-backit gull
rose in my mind,
darkly on the brightness of that day,
and bitterness and hatred lay
under their veering shadows,
and I heard again the stabbing epithets
of farmers and hill-weathered shepherds
coming at me with a tired insistence,

turned aside and hollow till this day:
'vicious...wicked...evil...'

I could have dropped a boulder
on his head and ended there
the languor of his dying,
but his mother's face
was in my eye, enduring
all my fumblings with a mute reproach;
and I told myself the lie
that, after all, there might be hope:
*he is not blind, he'll walk again.*
The truth is that I could not end a life.

I kindled fire, supped tea
and ate, but the peaceful heart
of the day had turned
black in the clasp of my brooding.
I passed him on the journey out;
a final look, the one that shamed me.

Before the light has deepened
and the dipping of the sun
smears west with evanescent wounds
all will be, out there,
as it was before
I brought my burden of compassion
down through the glen of stones;
and the hoodies and black-backit gulls
will have his eyes
and steaming entrails,
and what remains
a fox by night will drag away.


*At Craigaig sheep-fanks, 3 June 1989*

# Crossing a Field, Knockbay

Dead tree and ruined house together
leafless, roofless in a world
from which a shining feather
to an outer abyss hurled

would merely falter to the ground
the fillet of some gentle dream
a crown of buds worn all around
children splashing in the avid stream

but light there's more of light
bare branches hold no shade
rooms darken only in the night
where even time has languished and decayed.

\*

# Bog-cotton

Sage-like, your white heads nod,
as though you were discussing the Universe or God
from your lowly station in oozing bogland
but I believe there's more you understand

of sun and rain and night and wind, than I;
and if the minuscule space you occupy
is all that the world has given you
summer on summer your sage heads nod anew.

*for Bill Henderson*

# Sloe-gathering

I found a new serenity
deep in the Valley bottom
squelching dusk on dusk
on the edges of the flower-dead marsh
alone but for a chiding bird,
a drifting owl or people heard.

As I picked the blackthorn berries
how intimately strange they seemed
with fleshiness affixed to wood
now that I, desirous of them,
was seeing them and grasping them
as though for the first time ever;

and the twisted trees forlornly spiked
seemed for the first time to become
sure individuals as the dark
came seeping through the Valley
sending me away and leaving
the trees where they have always been.

I have carved a valley in my mind
and go there when the notion takes me
to be in silence and in shade
with trees benignly crowding
as I gather yielding globe on globe
till those remaining have become
the very darkness.

# Late Harebell on Black Rock

November harebell, blue in the grey wind,
scrap of the summer that is gone;
if you had words for your survival
in the crack of a cold rock alone
I would not heed them, for the marvellous
may deviate from nature's law;
it is enough to find you set
a jewel on winter's withered claw.

*

# Mosaic

From all the china fragments
I have gathered in my years
of prowling round deserted habitations
kicking down molehills and picking over
the exposed earth of middens
some day a mosaic will materialise
when I take to the floor and surround
myself with a thousand pieces.

These will resolve themselves into
the image of a ploughman steering
a beautiful ship of horseflesh and iron
through a breaking sea of the earth
with the sun about to set itself
in the six red shards from Cashan.

*Postscript*

## I Shall Never Get Rich

I shall never get rich at this
business of trawling poems
from the silt of the hundred lives I've led
and the hundred thousand dreams

that ran like films
in the Odeon of my head
while I was sleeping
and closer to the dead

than any conscious state
could draw me; and here's an image
of a boat — beyond normality
of land, on the edge

of the deep and mysterious
towing a bag of holes —
and a prayer for golden coins to fall
from the slit guts of eels.

A NOTE ON THE TYPES

The inner text of *A Night of Islands* is set primarily in
Miller, designed by Matthew Carter and released in 1997.
It is a 'Scotch Roman', and follows the original style in
having both roman and italic small capitals. The style was
developed from types cut by Richard Austin between 1810
and 1820 at the Edinburgh type foundries of Alexander
Wilson and William Miller. The companion face, used for
the glossaries, is Trade Gothic Next, type designer Tom
Grace's attractive reworking of Trade Gothic, widely used
as a sans serif companion to a variety of serif typefaces.